Journey

to the

Heart

For Johnathan
with love to you;
Heartfully!
Valerie Diker
9/92.

Journey to the Heart

Valerie Diker

Illustrations by
Barbara J. Roman

Philosophical Library

I waited patiently for the Lord
and He inclined His ear...
He set my feet upon a rock
making my footsteps firm.
He put a new song in my mouth,
a song of praise to our G-d.

Psalm 40

ISBN 0-87131-718-4
Copyright 1992 by Valerie Diker, New York, N.Y.
For information write to M. Evans & Co. Inc.,
216 East 49 Street, New York, N.Y. 10022
Manufactured in the United States of America.

For
Valerie R. Clifton
My special friend in matters of the heart.

Thank you for sharing my journey,
and teaching me
by your life, how to live
in the heart of G-d.

Preface

It is an extraordinary gift when one person allows another to share in the intimacy of his/her spiritual quest.

I have been the recipient of just such a gift from Val Diker. Her spiritual journey began many years ago and has run like a powerful river, reshaping elements in the environment which surrounds it and undergoing subtle but significant changes as it rushes forward.

Her spiritual poetry, as represented in this collection, provides the opportunity for many other people to share in the feelings and the thinking which have so animated her progressively more intimate relationship to the world of transcendence.

What characterizes this journey? What is there to be discovered by the sensitive reader in the immersion in these poetic waters? Firstly, there is Val's special sensitivity to the presence of G-d in every minor shift in time and space. Her capacity to perceive holiness in both time and space is prodigious, and can open the reader to an infinitely more subtle awareness of the transcendent, within what appears outwardly to be totally mundane, devoid of sanctity.

Secondly, Val Diker has an extraordinary capacity for the portrayal of intimacy. With few words, her poems evoke powerful awareness of the capacity of the individual for interchange with G-d — an interchange which is both honest and reverential, both earthy and ethereal.

Thirdly, these poems embody a deep commitment to law as love. Rather than dichotomizing these two essential components of religious life, Val manifests in the written word that which is so abundantly clear in her daily life — that G-d's law is a manifestation of His love, and that his love is best reciprocated through the loving adherence to his law.

Val has engaged in a prodigious struggle to learn, and to live the Truth which she learns. Her journey to the heart is expresseed not only in her poetry but in her life.

There is much to learn and much to feel in reading these pages.

Saul J. Berman
Stern College
The day after
Simchat Torah 5751.

Contents

Struggling

Finding the Way

Prayers and Conversations

Realizations

Ecstasy

Introduction

People don't talk about G-d very much, especially Jewish people. They talk about a way of life—history, laws, customs— but not about how they feel spiritually. My friends, my family, my teachers, even my Rabbis, were scarcely able to share their personal feelings. I turned to books, and sought, with little success, others who could share their feelings. As my own spirituality began emerging, I was unable to ignore the stirrings of my soul and I began to write my own sentiments and to find solace by reading them often. Poetry objectified my feelings: it confirmed and validated them. Where did these powerful feelings come from? How did they emerge? I seek to share that with you now.

Many people turn to spirituality when their lives become unmanageable. Burdened with physical or emotional trauma, they turn to G-d. I turned to G-d when my own world was full—filled with worldly pleasures which no longer satisfied my deeper needs. Married, secure, successful: wealthy husband, healthy children; with all of this I felt an emptiness. In the fullness of my life an abyss was opening. I had what many desired; still I felt a void I could not understand.

Born to parents who were second and third generation Jewish Americans, living in a large city, I grew up in a home where religion was never discussed. No Yom Kippur, no Passover, no traditions, no prayers. We learned old-fashioned American ethics: honesty, achievement, manners, order in our lives, cleanliness, and above all, nothing in "excess."

As a child I learned Catholicism from Tessie the maid, and Mademoiselle took me to Mass. During the second world war, our family's concern was about the German occupation of France. The holocaust was not discussed. I gave up candy for Lent and bemoaned my unsmudged forehead on Ash Wednesday. My Easter basket overflowed. Each Christmas, my parents bought the biggest tree on the block. I never heard of Chanukah.

When I was seven, my brother became a Bar Mitzvah in a Reform ceremony. The memories linger.... his arguments with my mother, her prodding him to prepare, his lack of interest, hundreds of thank-you notes. The day itself labored on. Judaism was not discussed again.

When I was 28, my father died. The funeral was held in a Reform temple because it was the only place large enough to hold the 2000 people who came. Kaddish was not recited. It was the second and last time I ever entered a temple with my mother.

I didn't think much about being Jewish again until my eldest son turned thirteen. I had no wish to repeat the sham of my brother's experience; however, my husband persisted and I agreed. On the day my son became a Bar Mitzvah, a tiny flame ignited in me.

August of that same year, I accompanied my husband to Israel. It was a time of political upheaval. Invited by the mayor of Jerusalem, we stayed at the King David Hotel while Henry Kissinger negotiated the Sinai. It was a week that changed my life; I came home concerned and proud to be a Jew.

I began travelling to Israel twice yearly to fulfill philanthropic and social obligations; the Israel I knew was secular. Inevitably, however, I began meeting surviors of the holocaust who had remained observant. I was fascinated. Why? How? What was it that kept them faithful? I needed answers that they were unprepared to verbalize. I began to seek more specific Jewish experiences. I saw the hill where Saul fell, mortally wounded. I stood by the brook where David took his stone and slew Goliath. I attended services.

A wise woman in Jerusalem spoke to me one day of prayer. We did a visualization in which I saw myself praying. Alone in a desert cave, I "spoke" with G-d and gained a new awareness. This "waking dream" remained

with me for months. When I returned to America, I felt
driven to discover more about the powerful world of prayer,
to learn the active faith which had sustained the Jewish
people for over 4,000 years. I studied privately and in class;
I attended different synagogues. I struggled for hours with
the Hebrew liturgy until one Rosh Hashanah a fellow
congregant took pity on me. In one afternoon, he taught me
the Hebrew alphabet. Soon I "broke the code" and slowly
I began to read. I hired a Hebrew teacher, and learned the
sweet side of Torah from Hasidic Rabbis. Within weeks I
realized that the religion I sought was a way of life, not an
intellectual exercise; I knew I must reshape my lifestyle
around Judaism. This came as a surprise to me and as more
than a surprise to my family.

From these acts came enhanced commitment. Every
week was a new unfolding of knowledge and treasured
understandings. Every day brought a new way of being, of
dealing with issues thoughtfully and intentionally. I gained
a different perspective in which I was no longer the center
of my world. Rather, I was a crucial part of a larger, G-d-
centered universe, a world with purpose beyond human
ambition; a world ordered by faith, in which people could
be open, honest, responsive. Fragments of feelings, murmurs
of the heart threw my inner life into kaleidoscopic patterns.
I was dazzled by the colors, touched by emerging truths.

My search for spiritual intimacy continued; but I
was unprepared for the intensity of the moment when I
first felt G-d's presence. It happened in the exquisite
solitude of the New Mexican desert. There, in the silence
of prayer I experienced G-d.

Since then my life could be compared to a narrow gauge railroad on which I travelled in Peru from Cuzco to Machu Pichu. Leaving the station, the tiny train coughed silver smoke, lurched forward, jerked back, then abruptly jumped ahead. Laboriously it gathered speed, puffing its way up the treacherous Andes Mountains. We had been warned the night before, over tea, not to be alarmed when the tiny train stopped suddenly, rolled backwards, switched tracks, and began again its steady climb.

This experience clatters on in my memory as I continue my spiritual journey. I live that halting pattern: prodigious forward energy, abrupt stops, backsliding, switching paths, resumed progress towards that place of peace. My poetry is that journey.

Surely I know that G-d is everywhere, especially when the heart is open. Now I am determined to preserve the intimacy and clarity I felt in the desert, to live each day with the challenge of mindfulness and simplicity, preserving a sense of His nearness, allowing His light to reflect in my life. May the experience of G-d's nearness fill the consciousness of all who pray. May it surround, comfort, and inspire us to turn our lives into a perpetual prayer.

V.T.D.

Acknowledgments

With gratitude to my teachers and Rabbis who guided me on my journey. Particular thanks are due to Rabbi Shlomo Riskin for his faithful friendship and wisdom; to Rabbi Saul Berman for the depth of his listening, his teaching, and for sharing with me his passion for Torah; to Rabbi Shmuel DeShan, always near when spiritual and intellectual needs were great; and to Rabbi Adin Steinsaltz, present for me at my spiritual beginning and along my way, he warned me with a twinkle in his eye, "never trust a Jewish intellectual" and he blessed me "on the way...to search, to stray, and to find." My abiding gratitude also to the late Abraham Joshua Heschel for his inspiring thoughts which I have used to introduce each section.

Thanks beyond measure to my teacher and role model Judy Geldzahler. Patient, encouraging, my "Biblical Encyclopedia," Judy made observant Judaism accessible, easy, and natural for me. Thanks to my dear friend and personal editor, Kate Barton, whose love affair with G-d and with language helped make this book vibrant and true. Thanks also to Mary Wadkins, my assistant, whose endless search for detail and accuracy made the preparation of this book exciting and thoughtful.

V.T.D.

Journey

to the

Heart

Illusions

"Helpless and incongruous is man with all his craving,
with his tiny candles in the mist."

Boxes

All my life is tied in boxes
Filled with ancient things.
Years and years of bits and pieces
Saved so carefully.

A list, a map, a tattered stub
A little love saved up
Desperately in case there's none
In time, for me.

Letters punctuate the years
With longing to connect.
Furtive words of my desire
Fill the yellowed pages.

Pictures posed carefully
Orchestrate a dream—
Lasting only long enough
To snap the shutter closed.

All my life's in boxes
Strewn across a littered room.
Piled high with expectations
Aging, hopeless, unexplored.

Who will take these boxes
Stuffed with wishes unfulfilled?
They clutter the landscape
Of my empty life.

Illusions

The illusions by which we live
Lead to loneliness and loss of self.
The tragic need to feel
In control of emptiness.

The dreams we fold around
Ourselves to form an outer vision
Leave us gasping for a truth
On which to base decisions.

The myths we elevate to truth
Perpetuate our lies;
Deceiving needs to which we cling
Bind us to our false desires.

Visions in an imperfect mirror
Reflect our self-deception;
Distorted images, believed,
End in ceaseless repetition.

Death of Dreams

What is this life?
So pained and fragile,
A river overflowing its banks
Seeping out, flooding the fields
With life unlived, uncherished
Leaking out, wasting away.

Our dreams are dying
Lost in the unused life.
The hopes born in our hearts
Pour out through rusty pipes.

Drop by drop, tear by tear
All the years of silent desires—
We're all dying
Stuck inside our empty lives.

The unused life evaporates
Barely moistens the parched soil
Which holds the seeds of our dreams.
We're dying,
Dying of a withered heart.

The Juggler

The juggler stands with painted face
Her sad eyes hidden in the laugh lines
Drawn upon the dead white mask.

The juggler moves on nimble limbs
Shifting six batons
Rhythmic, slowly gathering speed
She spins and twists, barely balanced
Switching hands precariously.

The juggler tries to tempt and please
Smiling relentlessly.
Fearful, lest her mask slip
Revealing naked sadness.

Poor Fly

Poor fly
Destined to buzz
Endlessly through life,
Unable to alight and
Interrupt his flight
Even for a moment,
Poor Fly.

Slave to his instincts,
Surely G-d has given him
Some purpose for his
Buzzing;
Someday maybe
He will stop,
Poor fly.

Sometimes the contours
Of this world
Stop him
And he is knocked
Senseless,
Only to resume
His flight
As soon as he is able,
Poor fly.

Even you and I
Who have the choice
Seem inclined
To buzz around
And fly forever,
Poor flies.

The Day She Died

While I was busy
Death slipped in.
Quietly,
Without a sound
Death came round
And walked right in.

While I was busy
With endless issues
Of my life
Silently, unannounced
Death stepped in.

A stranger who
Never rang the bell.
While I was so busy
With my life—
Death appeared
And walked right in.

There was no time
There never is
The time is never right.
I'm always too busy
But death doesn't know—
As it slowly slips inside.

Silently we sit together
Death and I,
Asking unmasked questions.
And still I'm too busy
To wrestle with answers.
And then death smiles
And waits.

Sadness

Oceans of tears swell in turmoil
Deep, deep, the undercurrent pulls,
Insistent, merciless,
As if to tear the life from me.

Mocking sounds of an ocean
Drone in my fevered head
Jerking me roughly
Rocking, relentless,
Till I feel my frame will break.

With outside stress
And inside anguish
Tossing me across the waves,
I find no rest, no relief,
Only deep, deep sadness.

Frozen Daffodils

The north wind blows fiercely
Interrupting spring,
Iced apple blossoms
Bend in its path,
Daffodils frozen
Rigid with fear.

The north wind whistles
Interrupting spring,
Trembling tulips
Drop their petals
Leaving stamens raw, exposed.
Trusting blossoms, thrust back to winter
Vulnerable, frail, unsuspecting
Forced from spring's protective cloak.

Sad, those yellow daffodils.
Emerging now in trust,
Standing unprotected
In the wayward warmth of spring.

Like those glorious first flowers
Bursting from the fertile earth
I felt a fleeting moment
Of warmth and gentle nurture.

Standing tall and open
I saw their fragile strength
Succumb to winter's bitter wind;
Numbed by an unforgiving gale,
Closed up, faded, shriveled.

How to live with nature's whims?
When to trust nature's promise?
To curl up, crumple and die
Or bloom again in lingering doubt?

Fortified

How strong we think we need to be
Fortified with iron.
Sharpened spear prepared to strike,
If only we were not so frightened.

Scared, sad, trying desperately
To be the center of our world.
When all we need to do is look,
To see that someone else's hand
Has formed our universe already.

Summer House

I feel as cold as a summer house
Shivering in winter's chill;
Windows whine and shutters moan,
Unfastened by the restless wind.

I feel as cold as an unused oven
With no crusty bread rising inside;
As hollow as an emptied chest
No longer holding cherished things.

I feel as still as airless rooms,
Left cruelly unattended,
Unsecured, life suspended
When summer ended that year.

A house that lost its purpose
When its family disappeared,
No longer bursting with the cries
Of grief, surprise, delight.

Perched silent on the dunes,
Emptiness fills my dusty rooms;
Oh to feel Your loving grace
Come to claim forgotten spaces.

Changing Paths

*"New insight begins when satisfaction ends and all that has
been seen, said, or done looks like distortion."*

Enter Thou My Life

Enter Thou my life, O G-d,
Uplift me in simplicity,
That I may enter the sublime,
And know Thy grace beyond all power.

Enter Thou my life, O Lord,
And I in turn will turn to Thee.
Bring me close to what Thou lovest
Lead me to Thy perfect truth.

Hear the longing of my heart
To form a living covenant,
To know at last Thy countenance
And bask in the nearness of Thy Self.

Enter Thou my life, O G-d,
Teach me Thy holy thoughts.
Reach for me as I surrender,
And commit myself to Thee.

Wanting Not to Want

Wanting not to want
Is not a distant hope;
It is a new reality
   shining through layers of
      my emerging faith.

Wanting not to want
Inspires simple choices;
Desiring to live with less
   frees me from
      the tyranny of things.

Wanting not to want
Means letting G-d choose;
To use me as I am
   to celebrate
      my becoming.

Wanting not to want
Brings clarity and focus;
The breath of holiness
   glowing in a lifetime
      of truth.

Unlock My Heart

Dear G-d,
Unlock my heart.
Let my words be uplifted through
The power of my prayers as
My soul ascends the heights.
Then will I know oneness.

I am an empty vessel,
Fill me with Your light.
I stand before You
Clothed only in consuming love.
Rapt in awe, inwardness, and silence
I offer You my prayers.

Feverish Night

Slowly slow
I felt the air
Passing wordless by my flesh.

Quiet and still
I heard the air
Surround my fevered body.

Hair by hair
I felt the air
Pass over heated pores.

Slowly sure
I heard the moments
Parade endlessly by
Knowing I would never
Feel the same sensations.

Dark and slow I felt the moments
Marching by in measured pace.
The cool air prickling
My fevered flesh.

Life abundant,
Oozing out.
Thermostat no longer
Working. I know that I
Will never know
All the things I need to know
To keep the life alive
Inside of me.

How to hear Your constant voice
How to know Your healing,
How to feel in the stillness
That which I know
Moment to moment
Is mine.

Dawn Pilot

Dawn pilot writes in scarlet
Upon the lazy morning sky
Like an oriental brushstroke
Streaking by.
High at the left
Low on the right
What coded system breaks this night?

Slowly the streak slips away
Behind the deep grey mountains,
Too soon to know the full desire
Of its morning message.
Silent words, written in smoke,
Only the Captain of this ship
Knows what they wish
For me.

Now they've passed
Forever in the mist.
Even my eager heart
Can not insist
On one more glimpse.

So I'm left to wander
Through life's complex maze.
Slowly choose my way
Through the haze
Of uncertainty,
Trying to decipher
Your scarlet message.

Letting Go

Even stars
    Must let go of the heavens
        and fall.

So, too, must I let go of all
The things I thought that
I could not survive without.

The lining of my pockets
Is now turned inside out;
The crumbs have tumbled to the ground
And I stand before You
Unpretending.

I feel Your breath upon me
So close, this moment of release,
I trust that I could touch Your sleeve
If I reached just a little higher.

Then I could hear the whisper
Of Your welcome words
Bidding me come closer —
In the lightness of my letting go.

Waking Prayer

The insistent beep
Of my tiny alarm
Awakens me from
Slumber—
The dead sleep
Into which I have
Fallen.
Now is the time
For prayer.

Resistant,
I struggle to release
My body from its slumber.
And beg You Lord,
Restore my soul.

Eager to enter the
Daylight breaking
I dedicate my waking hours
To You, my gracious King.

As I stumble from my bed
Unsteady from the dreaming night,
I see the light of dawn
Beginning
To become the day.

My day, today
To seek and find
All that's there for me:
The beauty, the love, the nearness,
To You my G-d,
Today.

This Mourning

White wings of dawn
Stretched across this morning
Bring me insight.
So many questions
Need a knowing answer.
So many arrows in my heart.

Help me pierce the numbness
That denies feeling.
Life decisions, elusive and unclear
Seek a signal
To untie the knot.

White wings of dawn
Carry me to clarity.
Be for me a shaft of light
In the darkness of unknowing;
Speak honestly to my heart
This mourning!

Sabbath Child

Child of clay
Do not sleep this day away
You have wrestled with the angel
And gained his trust.
Do what you must
To make it holy.

Child of earth
Worthy to rule all creation
Blessed are you and chosen,
Come now, claim your birth.

Child of spirit
Infused with gifts of
Heaven and earth.
Set your heart upon desire and
Choose the way of holiness.

Child of hope
Standing at the gateway
Of completion
Dip your cup into the spring
And drink the wisdom of His love.

Child of soul
Feel the glowing gaze of G-d
Beyond the life of thought and will
Hear His voice inside the stillness
Know you hold His secret.

Child of G-d
Assail the limits of this world.
Invade the mystery deep within
And know the nearness of eternity.

New Found Wings

Dear G-d,
Support my fledging efforts
To fly on new found wings.
My heart is overflowing
Soothe my searching soul.

Support my faltering efforts
To live in Your perfection
To know the full dimension
Of Your demanding law.

Lord, I strive to know Your way,
To walk along Your path,
To feel the full intention
Of Your commanding love.

Chat with G-d in a Velvet Night

Blackest night.
No wisp nor curl of cloud
Nor star disturbs
The inky sky.
No moon to light
My faltering steps
On a changing
Path.

Cloudless sight
The jet sky obscures
All possibilities
To guide and lead
Me on my way.
Heavy skies
Wet with unshed tears
Do you conceal the wisdom
Of passing years?

No image here
Of mountains,
No outline of the hills,
No hope to help
Decipher
The mystery of Your will.

Blackest night
Telling me to wait
Go slowly
And reflect.
To let my prayers
Express the wishes
Of my heart:
To live what
I already know
In simplicity.

To choose wisely
To follow Your
Basic intention.
Velvet night
Your shadow obscures,
Forces introspection.
To make a connection
At the deepest level
Of my knowing.

I am here Lord
Listening
What is the wisdom
Of Your heart?
Will You fill
My heart
Till there is room
For nothing more?

Through my life Lord
I seek to live
Your will.
Help me to know
The path.
To define myself
In Your law
And Your love.

I am listening Lord
Although no image appears
My vision is clear
And I hear You
In the blackness
Of this velvet night.
Knowing, in faith, Lord
You are near me
Always.

Amen.

Under Taos Skies

Gentle break of Sabbath morn
I lie awake and worship
Under warming skies of dawn
The crow of a boasting cock
Declares this day begun.

Sharp yelps of playful pups,
Sheep bleating in the meadow,
Neighbor's truck racing by —
All seem softer, slower now.

Nothing to make
   Nowhere to go
      Nothing to want
Only to know, we have it all:
It is a holy day, today.

A day for intention
     Purpose and sharing
A time to be mindfully,
     Prayerfully present,
 To celebrate: Shabbat.

Walking to Shul In the Snow

Every step I choose to take
Makes an imprint
On the frozen path.
Giant steps in virgin snow,
Solitary steps sinking
Deep into the unbroken surface.
White crust yields to
The weight of my desires.

Virgin steps
Where none have trod before.
This is my path
Chosen carefully,
With clear intention
And trust
That there will always be
Solid ground
Beneath my feet,
To support my fledging stride.

Slow and steady
I venture forth,
In rhythm with the flow
Of all creation
I open myself to G-d
And to the world.

Sparkling snow!
I trust my G-d
That You will show me
Where to tread
And I will stride out
With hope
Seeing Your footprints
Just ahead
In the soft, white
Landscape of the spirit.

On the Road

The trees
Bow to each other.
The mountains
Bare their rainbow breasts.
Painted bands
Of yellow, green and grey
Unfurled
A world ablaze with color!

Thank you G-d
For Your earthly gifts:
The echo in the valley
The voice of the cliffs
The monumental vista just ahead.

The river
Spreads its winding arms
And welcomes me.
The narrow road
Beckons me to pass,
Bids me hasten on my way
To prayer.

Driven
To come before You
To stand in Your path,
I feel Your commanding
Presence, on this road.

Changing Paths

Today is the day my life begins
When I shall live in a desert that blooms.
  My desert is a state of being
  Not an emptiness filled with diversions
  Or a setting for restless desire.
It is a state of soul
Whose silence vibrates with life.

Let not the comfort of cherished habits
    turn my head;
Or self-centered tranquility
    numb my spirit.
Keep me in the service of Your love
    O my G-d
That I may lift my desire to
    A higher Truth.

Loosen the bonds that bind my spirit
That I may know where You want me to go.
Let my need for You order my arrangements,
Obedience serve as my brake.

Defend the frontier of my desert!
It is pure and it purifies.
Protect the sacred silence of my heart
That I may penetrate
The sanctuary of my soul.

Struggling

"Why, we often ask in our prayers, hast Thou made it so
difficult to find Thee?

Touch Me Silver

Grey dawn
Heavy with tears
Weep with me this morning.
Silver skies
Clouded and unclear
Speak to me
With words of scarlet
Emblazoning the day.

If only I could see
Your message
Written in the darkened sky.
Though the dawn
Is pierced with light,
Bright with hidden wisdom,
Still my heart languishes
Unenlightened.

Touch me silver,
Mother of pearl,
Rubies set in golden light.
Teach me sapphire,
Tourmaline and crystal
Tell me why I suffer so
And still I fail to see
Your message written
In the sky for me.

Teach Me to Forgive

Dear G-d,
Surely Thou hast kissed the mountains,
  stroked the skies with color,
    and painted them with rainbows
Touched the tops of the still small trees,
  and with Thy holy breath,
    made them to sway softly.
Teach me to forgive!

In the beauty of Thy creation
  which moves me to awe
    should be the lesson how to live
      in harmony and love.
Teach me to forgive.

Lord, I wash Thy feet with tears
  of my humility;
I stand before Thee
  waiting for Thy word.

As my bones begin to mend,
  my body slowly strengthens;
    help me heal my broken heart.
Teach me to forgive.

To love when nothing loves,
  To cherish that which seems uncaring,
    To live with open heart,
Teach me to forgive.

Fullness of Faith

Lord do not hide Yourself from me.
Receive me in the truth of my intention
Accept me in the fullness of Your love.
There is no space empty of Your glory.

Be for me a font of holiness
Touch me with the passion of Your truth.
Though I am imperfect
   a fragment of Your oneness,
Hear me
   Heal me
    Hold me
In the shadow of Your grace.

The impulses of my heart are pure
The desire of my spirit burns
   To know You,
    To serve You
In truth and understanding.

Lord do not hide Yourself from me
In the essence of my humanness
I yearn for You to crown with glory
My simple life of faith.

Your Constant Gift

Dear G-d
Melt my frozen heart
Thaw my rigid soul
Return to them human feeling.
Bring them slowly back to life.

Promise they will know again
The fullness of intended love.
Without the death of isolation
That stills my halting pulse.

Without the dread of disappointment
That froze my hope, so long ago.
The searing cold of isolation
That left my spirit undefended.

Bring me to believe again
It's safe to feel the pain.
To know the passion of Your love
Will lead me to that place of peace
Where I'll receive Your constant gift:
My humanity.

Spill Out in Beauty

White fire flashes the mesa
Lightning streaks across the flat.
Thunder rumbles; the moon glows
Its searching light illumines
My garden.

Grey blue sky, burdened with rain
Wrinkled brows these twilight hours,
Save for the shining, silver clouds
Which keep the storm away.

Lord let my desire
To know Your myriad ways
Be not lost in searching,
Or submerged in storms of doubt.

The fire of my yearning
Will burn the clouds away,
Until I learn to hear You clearly
Until I know Your way.

Then will my garden sparkle,
Each flower burst with life.
Then will Your seed inside
Spill out in beauty
Showering my world
With hope.

My Truth

O G-d
Strengthen my mind and heart
That I may know and understand
The mysteries of Thy universe.
    Allow me to decipher
    The lessons there to learn.

The faith to embrace
The belief which emerges:
Thou art the first, the last and
Always will be my truth.
    How can I fear, who will turn my head
    With slick talk and practiced phrases?

Thy truth is slowly understood,
Fruit weighing succulent on the vine.
The sweetness of Thy words intoxicates.
    Lingers, luminous
    Transcendent.

Oh let Thy face shine forth;
Brightening my way.
Then will I know Thy nearness,
Thine ear receive my voice.
    Then will I hear Thee clearly
    Glowing in faith's choice.

Two Lovers

Weeping
Pea soup sky
This morning.
Blue fog
Heavy with tears
Rolls off the mountains—
Folds around my slowly
Beating heart.

Sleeping skies
Weeping for my sorrow.
My spirit shrieks through
Layers of conflicting needs.
My soul shrinks in anguish.

Hear me G-d!
I'm here, I'm whole.
I need to be known
In the chambers of heaven
Before I grow too old to bear
The tearing of two lovers
Fighting for my soul.

Prayer of Arrival

Dear G-d,

Slow my racing heart,
Calm my crowded mind,
Ease my estrangement,
Soothe my aching soul.

Help me heal the rupture
In my life of prayer.

Stay near me Lord,
Hear my distress.
Help me bridge the chasm
Of my loneliness.

Soothe my tired spirit.
Stop my killing pace.
Show me how to rest
In the stillness
Of Your grace.

Weep, Willow, Weep

Weep, willow, weep.
Drop your tears into the pond
And when the pond has overflowed,
Carry them in the clear rushing brook
Back to the source of all beginnings.

Weep, willow, weep.
Let the tears of ages fall
Into the stream that cleanses the earth
Of memories and searing pain
Of lost desires, hopes unmet.

Weep, willow, weep.
As I pour my scalding tears
Into the coolness of the brook.
"...Like a doe crying out for running water,
So longs my heart for Thee..."

Weep, willow, weep,
Into the silent still of spring.
My grieving tears wash my wounds,
Spill into the river whose streams make glad
The golden city of G-d.

Weeping willow o'er the pond
Rooted in eternity,
Absorb the tears which pour out
Of my faint and aching heart.
I will drink from the wellspring
Of His love.

Phoenix

Arise Phoenix,
Again and again
Lift your weary frame.
Slowly, stiffly
Raise your head.
Let your earthbound nature follow
Your spiritual desires.

Arise Phoenix,
Bloated and grotesque
From the sickened throes of death.
Anguished, injured
Weighted down
Prepare yourself to
Fly once more,
Phoenix.

Arise.
The soul will follow.
Do not lie there
Layered in the dust
Choking, groping
Exploding in disgust.
Elevate yourself
Lift your weary wings
See the others who succumbed
Lying there helpless
Inhaling the dust.
Weak, vapid
Gasping for air
Barely breathing.

Arise Phoenix,
Again and again.
Feel the life
Beating gently,
In your faithful heart.

Arise Phoenix,
Don't give up.
Trust that your desires
Will be met
One by one
Somehow.

Great bird
Gift of G-d
Do not lie there in the dust.
Your heart
Beats still
In your weary frame.

Arise Phoenix
Show your strength
And live again.
Break the fetters
Which bind your soul
And struggle on
In faith.

Longing

Do You know my thoughts Lord?
Do You know how I long for You?
       My soul cries out,
           I languish alone,
               yearning for Your grace.

Happy is the soul who learns Your law
       You make him confident in Your ways.
Happy is he who seeks Your path
       His steps are sure and steady.

Teach me Lord,
       Touch me
           Show me Your way.

I cry out at night, hoping You will hear.
I am open Lord, yearning for Your care.
I am righteous Lord, do not abandon me.

Your mercy Lord comforts me.
Your goodness soothes my faltering spirit.
Who will rise up when dear ones
       do not understand?
Who will stay by when I am
       battered close about?

There is only One who hears
      the voices deep inside
Only One who listens to
      the longing of my soul.

I call to Thee Lord,
      hear my plaintive cry.
I look to Thy inspiration,
      Thou art my only guide.

Lead me Lord,
      Teach me,
Thou art my shining star.

When the world darkens and
      my path becomes obscure
I look to Thy holy light and my way
      is clear once more.

Sunrise on a Cloudless Day

Earth,
A luminous, white scrim on an empty stage—
Save one slim tree to delineate the foreground.
Ready for the dancer's entrance is
The dawning of this cloudless day.

Colorless sky, awaits the splash of daybreak,
Clear light,
Uncluttered stage,
Ready for the dance.

The undulating line of mountains
Poured across the bottom of the stage
Adds earthly detail to this airy setting.
Vibrating energy, backdrop for truth
The story will unfold.

Lord, be my director in this dance of life.
Show me my steps in the drama today.
I will follow You across the stage
Stopping on the crossmarks You have placed.
In faith I play my part
Against a simple scrim:
The luminous cloud of unknowing.

Trust Your Truth

Can I trust my own reality
Knowing G-d makes no mistakes?
He speaks to me from many places
Sometimes He surprises me
And speaks directly to my heart—

Trust your truth,
Your searching heart will find
Its answers in My time.
Allow My love to quiet you
Profoundly.

Trust your truth,
Each doubting breath you draw
Diminishes My giving
Denies your swift response.

Trust your truth,
My gift to you
It is My voice you hear,
Whispered from My Heart
Crying out in yours.

Finding the Way

"To animals the world is what it is, to man this is a world in the making, and being human means being on the way, striving, waiting, hoping."

Starry Night

O starry night, the firmament is
   pregnant with promise,
Thy seed is everywhere creating
   the heaving hills
The throbbing of the mountains
The pulsing of eternal hope.

Starlight pierces the firmament
   incandescent in the hills,
A touch of the untouchable,
   magic, diamonds, piercing moon,
Moving clouds, intense white light,
Oh the crystal crispness of this moment!

The world is shared creation,
   mortal and divine.
Help me understand the balance
   and know my chosen role.
Stars shimmer in the heavens;
Lights illuminate the earth.

Lead me,
   Guide me,
      I will follow.

Musing

Strengthen my emerging faith, O G-d.
Delicate as spring's first flower
Fragile as dew on a fresh blade of grass—
A sense of Your commanding presence
A knowing You are truly here.

In Your perfection, let me learn Your way.
Teach me, test me, draw me ever closer.
Encircle me when life presses in.
Be for me a crown of splendor—
Surround me with the fire of Your truth.

Erev Shabbat: Coming Home

Crimson sunset, a sliver of the moon
G-d's presence, His promise of
Earthly continuity.
The knowing that fills my heart
Is the trust, that in Him
There will never be a void.

Blazing sunset welcomes,
Pierces my heart
With the beauty of its being.
All of nature celebrates
My homecoming.

Flashes its coat of many colors
Against an endless backdrop
Of kissing mountains and Aspen trees
Reaching to touch the sky.

Echoing my yearning
To rest in Your peace
To cherish Your holiness
In my life.
These are the blessings of Taos.

Painted Sunrise

Sweet smell of lilacs intoxicates
Pastel haze whispers a new day dawning.

Cock on the hill softly crowing
Glowing light ignites the sky.
Birds sing their welcome chorus
Soloists trill triumphant.

Sharpened pencil line of light
Traces the mountains
Across the fertile valley.
Etched in the mist,
They lumber trunk to tail.

A sudden flash of tinted peach
Brushed in broad streaked strokes
Announces the emerging day.

The languid moon lingers, faithful,
Silent in the bluing sky.
Soft, the outline of layered hills
Emerges, as a photo gaining focus.

Thank You G-d for Your creation
Renewed once more this day.

Shabbos: Gift of Rest

Shabbos, Shabbos, day of rest
A holy time, wholly mine
Perfect as the chime of a crystal bell
Clear as my vision unclouded by doubts
A gift that is given to me.

A day to reflect, observe admire
A day to dream, to dare, to aspire
A law, a life, a truth that is higher
Than all that I have ever known.

Clear as the sky unpierced by clouds
The fragrance if roses dampened with dew.
Bright as the hope that grows with desire
Wrapped in a sense of awe.

A law, a life, a way that is sure,
A promise already fulfilled.
A day to dream and walk with angels,
A way to peace that is mine.

Maariv at the Wall

Soft, smooth stones cradle my aching head,
Caress my salty cheeks;
Warm sun streams at my back,
Golden rays cascade across my shoulders.
Hashem echad.

Birds trill their songs of praise
Triad of gladness fills today.
My heart opens to receive Your blessing
In this prayer-filled place.

Supported by the sun behind me
Ancient walls stand strong in front,
Their gentle curves receive my shape
It seems a perfect combination.

Lord, let my being blend formlessly
With Your endless truth,
My body melt in the yearning of my soul;
There is no beginning and no end.

Prayers of the ages uttered as at first
Filled with a sense of Your nearness,
The possibility of Your response.
Hear me Lord:

> *With everlasting love Thou hast loved the*
> *house of Israel.*
> *Thou hast revealed to us Thy laws.*
> *They are our life and the measure of our days.*
> *We will meditate on them day and night.*

Pray for the peace of Jerusalem.

Speak to My Heart

Speak to my heart O G-d.
Instruct me from an inner Sinai
To penetrate the holy of holies,
And find Your spirit deep within.

Speak to my heart O my G-d.
I am insatiable, for Your word.
The purer my readiness, deeper flows Your truth:
The sublime hearing is all.

> O let my soul be invaded by G-d,
> Flooded by His grace,
> Then will my spirit shine
> In holiness and faith.

Come close O G-d and form with me
A covenental group.
Stay near that I may always be
The instrument of Your design.

Speak to my heart O my G-d.
Touch me with Your wisdom.
Teach me to reach inside and find You
Flowing from my depths.

Speak to my heart O my G-d.
Teach me with tender compassion.
Let Your spirit fill my soul;
I seek You in the fullness of Your love.

Cinquains at Daybreak

Perfect
Stripe of color
Day glow peach greets the day
Steady flow of brilliant color
Constant.

Mountains
In black relief
Against the stripe of peach
Painted beneath an azure sky
Perfect.

Intense
Measured color
Dense brush, a steady hand
Paints the sky with pearly blush.
Glorious.

Clear hue
Precisely drawn
Steadfast as the new dawn
Mystic, breaking slowly, filled with
Your grace.

Lessons
Learned are many:
Wait, patient as the dawn
Go slow, reflect in beauty, change
Will come.

In faith
Trust G-d alone
Will light your special path,
Declare new ways to honor Him
In life.

Come Day

Come morning!
Lift the veil that
Night has spread
On my deeply
Dreaming bed.
Break day!
Chase away the
Spirits which filled
The darkened hours.

Let your power fade the moon,
Force the sun from
The horizon.
Fill the sky with
Morning light and
Clear the cobwebs
From my soul.

Come morning!
Bless this day.
Let my spirit shine
Fresh washed with
Morning dew.
Then I, as flute
Can play Your notes
In my own devoted way.
Come day!

Morning: Succot in the Jewish Quarter

Blue sky smiles through my latticed window.
Old city peeks through ancient, iron gates.
Slatted metal shutters reveal the panorama,
Domed roofs rising in softly
    carved curves.

The years roll away, history unfolds,
Portraits of the ages through my
    window panes.
Treasures of the ages, past my
    iron gates.

Cats yowl, memories echo,
    Minaret beyond
Belches out its urgent call to prayer.
Warm sun blesses this peaceful scene.

Succession of succahs lean on
    every level.
Sheeted sides, stars through the *schach*
Seasonal fruits dance from
    skylit roofs.

Pious voices praise in
    scattered booths,
Church bells toll the hour,
    Jerusalem awakes
To celebrate this joyous season.

Child of Light

I am Your child of light.
Sprung from the core of Eternal Being.
Seedling of Your perfect love;
Tender leaf turns to holy light.

A child of simple needs and pure desires
Soft spreading petals of a summer rose
Thirsting for the shower of Your love,
Reaching to receive Your tender care.

As Your child I bear witness to my roots
Receive the nurture of Your promise.
And I in turn will turn to You
With growing hope and blooming trust.

A Place for Me

A place to be is what I seek
A personal, a private space
To embrace my solitude
And be at one with Thee.

A place to be intensely me
In rhythm with eternity
A space to know Your vibrancy,
And dream Your dream for me.

A place for me is what I seek
To see the wonders You have wrought.
To feel the love You lavish
On those who reach and trust.

Each breath, each tear, each fervent prayer
Bids me listen, listen well.
Feel Your heartbeat telling me
To wait and seek, inside.

I know You're there, yet sometimes
How remote You seem to be.
Though You see me clearly
Jaded senses dulled by life
Betray my inner eye
And I have fallen back inside
The darkness of myself.

So now I seek that private space
Awaiting as I grow in faith
Until the world's conceits grow dim
Within my yearning heart.

Then I will know Your private grace
Becomes for me that sacred place,
The holy space that's left for me
To be at one with You.

My Completion

When through my tears
I count the years
Spent wandering
In search of my
Completion.

Then G-d came quickly
And placed His hand
Quiet upon my lips
Silencing
My guilty story.

Lovingly He helped me
Learn to pick myself up
And continue
Through the crippling
Doubt and fear
To victory: intimacy
My cherished friendship
With Him.

Weightless in Faith

Let me wade from the shore of
    earthly knowing,
Till my feet no longer touch
    the sands;
Till my spirit rises, weightless,
    my soul rests on the waves.

Let me rejoice in letting go,
Celebrate the lightness of release;
Floating in the waters
    of Your wisdom,
Supported by the strength
    of Your love,
Buoyant in the gift
    of believing,
Relying at last on You.

Motse Shabbat: Quiet Moments

Now in this silent hour
    when day separates from night
        I am surrounded by G-d.

Enpurpled clouds of evening
    wrap round glowing hills,
Rose-violet rays of sunset
    pierce the pulsing sky.
Portraits in nature pray the hymns
    to Him who fashioned all.

Now in this silent hour, I am
    radiant in recognition
That all which I behold
    reflects Your perfection.
Here in the desert shadows
    nature is as it issued from
        Your hands.

Now in this silent hour, I consecrate
    myself to You—
The source, the spirit, my inspiration,
    midst the glory of creation,
        I celebrate.

Hiking the Ski Valley Trail

Footprints on a dusty path
Leaving but a trace to mark
Where I have walked.
The wind whips past
Erasing the patterned place
Where I have trod,
Leaving a living heart print
Instead.

Heat of day beating down
Sucking moisture from the clay
Leaving dusty clouds about my feet
Where I have walked.
The dry earth chokes,
Hoping to replenish the nourishment
It seeks.

I seek to replenish.
My soul is parched, my heart thirsts
To leave a spiritual path
Where I have walked.
The wind shifts, fresh
Around my searching steps
As I stride out in quest
Of eternity.

Who will walk where I have trod
Amid the swirling sands?
Will they find my fragile path
Looking for Your truth,
Your spiritual imprint left
In trust?

Prayers and Conversations

"...possessed by an awareness of the nearness of G-d...as close as the throbbing of one's own heart..."

Love Me Lord

My G-d how I love You!
How many times
I weep for sweetness
When I feel You
Very close.
Yet how far I am from
Being truly Yours.
My desires are too easily
Distracted
For me to give myself
Entirely to You.

But I will seek Your inspiration
In my darkest hours
And in Your light will I emerge
Whole and searching, once again.
Freed from loneliness and isolation,
Basking in the nearness of
Your love.

So love me Lord, as I love You
Accept me in my weakness;
I will find my own uniqueness
In an instant of Yourself.
I am a spark of the Divine
And in that flash
Of recognition
I will find Holiness,
Knowing Your life resides
In mine.

Early Prayer

Lord, let the gathering strength
    of my own spirituality
    rise above tradition
        when tradition bogs me down.

Let my connectedness
    give me compassion
    for those with whom
        I can not share.

Lord, let Your strength
    flow through me
    rooting me firmly,
        as my spirit soars!

Grounded in time,
    focused on eternity,
    still my soul as my heart
        flies high in the heavens.

Erev Shabbat: Santa Fe

Tender hues of evening,
  Brushed effortlessly
    Across Sabbath skies.
Ribbons of rose
  Reaching forever
    Behind distant peaks.

Diaphenous silk
  Gently enfolds
    The rolling mountains.
Light of day
  Leaves its
    Lingering colors.
Energies subside,
  Sinking into
    Undulating hills.

Peace abounds
  Surrounded by the
    Fading beauty of day.
Folded into
  The silent darkness
    Of tonight.

Dear G-d,
  Faithful, watching,
    Always near.

Clearly You hover closely around
  In the majesty of Your creation,
    The beauty of Santa Fe.

Shabbat Shalom.

Shabbat: Queen of Days

Dear G-d,
It's all here,
Every hope, every dream
Every way in which we trust
Is contained in the Queen of Days:
Shabbat.

The idea, our inspiration
Each day, each week
Is to shorten the spaces
Between the moments
Of Your grace.

Finally to live
In one never ending moment
Of your perfect love.

Awake in Prayer!

Dear G-d
Pray me to simplicity.
Let me be the eye
Of Your intention.
The spark of Your divinity
Come to claim a
Holy place.
Pray me to simplicity
Today.

Let me be the vessel
For Your divine serenity—
The center of Your never ending
Peace.

Then I as Thy creation
Become a celebration
Of all that is holy
Perfect and pure,
Focused and free,
Joyful in Thee,
Pray me to simplicity
Today.

My Broken Heart

Oh G-d, do not be silent and still.
The birds call to one another
　　Even the tiny winged things
　　Murmur their coded message.
I call to Thee now from the depths
Of my broken heart
　　Hear me!

The song of the Bluejay issues forth,
The Robin trusts his sustenance awaits.
　　My sustenance is from Thee, oh Lord
　　I too wait, with hope.

Guide me,
　　Teach me,
　　　Show me
A path for today whose truth
Stretches out forever.

In the weakness of my broken bones
And the aching of my heart
　　I yearn to feel the warmth
　　Of Your healing.
I have emptied myself of preconceptions
And placed myself humbly in Your care.

With a trembling heart
I await Your words;
　　Share with me Your perfect wisdom;
　　Lead me to that tranquil place
Where I may know peace,
And find You in my heart.

　　　　　Amen.

Come Sweet Night

Come sweet night
As efforts of the day subside,
Drop your dusky mantle
On the silence of the stage.

Come sweet night
Gently brush the fires
Of this scorching day aside,
So all is still as
The silence of my prayer.

I ask You, G-d, to be with me
In the stillness of tonight;
Guide and keep me, faithful,
Until the daylight break.

Hushed sweet night
Deep and dark and dreaming
Velvet hours pass as moments
When my spirit rests in Him.

Sheltering night, don't linger long,
As light inspires dawn to break
And parts the sleeping clouds,
I claim my waking spirit.

Today in faith I will arise
And try anew to realize
The blessing of His plan.

Tisha b'Av Sunrise

The morning sky rolls over the rooftops
  Warming my searching soul
Silently it fills me
  With feelings of rebirth.

The strength of the sunshine
  The renewal it brings
Reminds me of Your promises
  So faithfully fulfilled:

Be to Me My people
  And I will be your
    G-d, King, Redeemer
Teacher of the lessons
  Of holiness and healing.

Merciful and giving
  Demanding and fierce
Jealous in My longing
  For your covenantal trust.

Know I'll not forsake you
   In your weakness and
      Temptation
Faithful to My promise
   Through the ages.

Love and fear and follow Me
   I'll defend you
      As Your Savior.

Forever My people,
   Remember My pledge
It is I who made it
   Directly to you.

Weary Traveller

Carry me, carry me *Hashem.*
Let me rest my weary soul,
As a child I ask of Thee
Carry me, *Hashem.*

Pray with me, say to me
Tender words of gentle strength
Till I rest awhile in Thee
Stay with me, *Hashem.*

Take my hand , touch my soul
Teach me all that I must know
To enter the garden of Thy love
Nourish me, *Hashem.*

Take my hand, hold my heart
Hear the longing of my spirit,
Teach me the wisdom of Your way.
Walk with me, *Hashem.*

My Renewal

O G-d,
Thou who has endowed our lives
With a ceaseless urge for harmony
My innermost being sings praises
    to Thy name.

Thou who daily renews creation
I look to Thee for my renewal.
And in the patterns of nature's change
I celebrate Thy glory.

Help me to trust
    That in Thy wisdom
        I will be sustained.

Fill me with Thy peace.
As water gushes from the rock
Pour forth Thy glory.
Nourish all who search for Thee—
I thirst for Thee in love.

Lord, I stand before You
Clothed in my desire
To know You in Your mystery
To love You in Your law.

Strength of the Stones

Standing behind me
As I stand before You
Unencumbered,
The strength of the stones
Surges through me.
Solid, cool, supporting,
As I press against them,
Sure as Your love
Strong as Your promise.

Blessed stones
Their timelessness
Reminds me of the
Master Builder,
Ever faithful.

Formed by the ages
Hewn by man
They echo
In every moment
The divine partnership.

Here in praise
I humbly raise
My heart to Thee
And gather my desires
Into one small word:
Hashem.

Then I become a
Living prayer
Knowing You are
Truly there
Listening, waiting,
Patient, for me.

Liquid Prayers

Tears are my liquid prayers of love,
Offered to You in my contrition,
Humility and recognition.
You are the light, my highest truth,
The Holiness for which I strive,
Fulfillment of my deep desire
for serenity.

Hear me, O my G-d
be near me,
precious Lord.

Help me live Your law with understanding,
To know Your statutes and commandments.
Tears are the fountain of my prayers
Cascading from an open heart,
Leading me, joyful, into Your presence.

Be with me
the only One
the Holy One I love.

My prayers splash silent in the dust
Honoring Your majesty
With all the life that's given me
Knowing I must cleave to You
and only You
in trust.

Farewell, Rabbi

Who now, Oh Lord
Will hold my soul
During its earthly quest,
To know Thy wisdom in my life
And find Thee in my heart?

Who now, Oh Lord
Will keep my mind
Clear and focused
Willing to absorb
All that thou would have me know
Who now, my Lord, who now?

I, my G-d, I alone,
Will keep my spirit open.
Till the knowing in my heart
Overcomes my yearning,
Till the glowing closeness
Fills my soul with You.

Night Prayer

Dear G-d,
Your arms, like the arms
Of a million stars
Reach out to me now.

Your breath, like the
Softest summer breeze
Dries my tears
And comforts me.

Your voice, like a willow
In a gentle wind
Whispers words of strength.
Your love, transcendent,
Fills me,
Sustains my life.

Your spirit, now
Entwined with mine
Inspires hope and courage.
Your soul infuses mine with life
So I can turn to You
And emulate Your holiness.

Prayer of the Heart

Lord, I stand before You,
    unadorned
        I seek your truth.

In silence and stillness
    I meditate.
In emptiness I cultivate
    expectation
        trust and joy.

Silence like the sunlight
    illuminates my path
As I deepen my life
    of prayer,
Permeate my being
    with Your presence.

I will always be
    a humble beginner
Exploring this process of
    perpetual surrender.

I seek the silence of the heart
    to know the mystery
        of Your love.

Realizations

"The ineffable has shuddered itself into the soul."

Wonder

Wonder is a sudden gift
   a rainbow or a star,
A miracle surprising
   the heart of a child.

Wonder is a gift of G-d
   Who lifts us to His vision
Who lends us His holy light
   to see His wisdom in our lives.

Wonder is His legacy
   His love to those who trust
That in His promise we will know
   the holiness we seek.

Wonder is a shining gift
   a moment touched with light.
When spirit overcomes the flesh
   and time stands still.

For Fiquet: At Dawn

Peach vapor rises from
Slowly spreading mountains
Reminding me — tread softly
On my journey of today.
Gentle steps thoughtful and sincere
Pondering life's richness;
The mystery of shifting feelings
Unknown treasures close behind
Dawn's softly spreading mountains.

Fortress

My desire to expand my world
Leads me to the edge
Of who I am.
Then love approaches,
Close with quiet steps
And tells me where
My freedom lies.

Not in worldly battles
Fought with intellectual swords
But in my inner fortress
Where love pierces the soul
And truth emerges.

Sunset: Holy Fire

Holy fire disappears behind
    quiet hills
Carnelian rays shoot horizontal
    flashes
Flames enshroud the jagged
    mountains.

Quiet air surrounds as
    heat of day subsides.
The glory of the painted skies
    sings Your praise,
Ever present, never repeating
    constant surprise.

The magnificience of this evening
    dazzles my ravished eyes
Which try in vain to capture
    Your mystic vision.

This magic sight defies
    the efforts
Of my hungry eyes
    to hold its glory
With precision.

Perhaps the mirror of
    the inner I
Will catch its searing
    beauty,
Filling my soul with a
    sense of awe
Always renewing, ever
    glorious,
This nightly celebration—
    a gift to all inspired by
The mystery of creation.

Shabbat Cinquains

Shabbat
Shelter of hope
Grateful joy peaceful prayer
Quiet space for slow reflection
In faith

Precious
Moments in time
Creative energies
Suspended in simplicity
And love

Awesome
Witness Your gift
For the chosen faithful
Remember and observe this day
In peace

Always
Cherish and keep
The laws He gave in faith
On the merits of our fathers'
Greatness

Preserve
The holiness
The sacred gift He gave.
This sense of everlasting peace
Is ours.

Words

Words
In their frailty
Fail in the
Final attempt at
Communication
With G-d.

In the attentive
Silence
Lie the secrets
Of true
Connection.

Not by knowing
But by love;
Not by doing
But by stillness

Comes
The trust
That G-d
Transcends
Words:

The faith
That He knows
And waits for us
Patiently.

Mountain Song

Painted shadows sketch the forms
Softened brushstrokes, mountains' song.
Molded masses shine in glory
Nature's story, G-d is here.

Ancient forms folded by time
Melt in the late day's light
Glowing in the dappled hills
Of greens and greys and purple.

Shaded skies of greys and blue
Celebrate stillness.
Nature's gift brings night anew
To this silent, fading day.

Rat-tail rainstorms
Gather in the distance
Rolling thunder rumbles, gently,
Far from my beating heart.

Joyous! This peaceful landscape
Glows in my gleaming eyes—
Stills my restless spirit,
Fills my overflowing heart
With awe, and knowing,
You are the Creator.

Face to Face

To meet G-d face to face
Is to turn life into
  One
    Eternal
      Moment of truth.
To contemplate truth
Leads us through fear
  Towards
    Ultimate
      Peace—
That place for which
Our world becomes
  A pallid
    Alternative.

Silent Prayer

Holiness—
Reach for it,
Wait for it
Open your heart.
Be fully present
In the moment.

Feel His love
Beckoning;
It lives in your soul.
Respond in certainty.

Feel the earth
Beneath your feet
As your spirit rises.

Offer yourself
As a gift to Him,
Trust the truth
Of the wordless
Dialogue.

In the silence
Is the sanctity;
Your search
Is ended.
          Amen.

Listen!

Draw near and listen
   To the silence of His voice.
Draw near in stillness
   The words are written in your heart.

Let your thoughts be measured
   And your words few.
Though the dream is elusive
   The silence is not empty.

Hear the fullness of His message
   The promise of each word.
Draw near and hear the silence.
   Listen!

Sunrise Signals

Soft wet sky, heavy with rain
Grey blue mass in the hills
Nestled in the curve of a single mound,
Neolithic form, hazy, subdued
The sunrise this morning whispers.

Small, white cloud, sparrow's wings
Glides above the southern range.
Signals distant greeting,
Listen to the message born.

Does it bid me tread easy
In the journey of my life?
Step softly, prayerfully
Barely leaving tracks.

Birds call to one another, listen!
Each sings a coded message
Cacophony of sounds
Blends in a symphony of life.

Each sings its soulful message
Meant for particular ears.
If I listen
Will I hear Your call?

In the valley a stray dog howls,
Greets the dreaming day.
Slow blend of earth and sky
Heralds Your glory.

Yours is not a clarion cry
The slightest hint suffices.
The subtle sounds of life on earth:
Your daily signal of rebirth.

G-d's Love

G-d's love consumes as
We reach out in faith
And touch Him deep in our soul.

My Faith

In the fullness of my faith
    I am free.
In the magic of its depth
    I will know glory.
The power of its history
    Ignites my eager heart,
The beauty of its intimacy
    Moves me to a lofty place.

I am G-d's holy mountain
His spirit lives inside;
Its radiance is mine to cherish
Filling me with hope and purpose.

My search is over
    Watchfulness prevails.
My G-d is not found in space or place
    But in the darkest regions of myself.
Receive the sanctifying grace He grants
    I will live His love.

I am free!
Bound only by eternal
    Privilege.
Golden threads
    Spun by angels,
Guide me to make
    The divine connection.
Seeking His promise
    Through prayerful acts
        And introspection.
In my faith at last, I am free.

The Heartbeat of a Holy Person

You can tell a holy person
By the way he ties his shoes.
The smallest things he does
In a wholly sacred way.

You can tell you're in the presence
Of a truly blessed person
By feeling the peace in his soul.

He has no wants that can't be filled
No restless needs for more.
He seeks not constant stimulation
Because he thrills in You.

You will know that one is holy
When you listen to his heartbeat,
Synchronized with heaven and earth
It beats in time with G-d.

A balanced way of gentle knowing
Glowing in its sufficiency,
Owing nothing to the world we know.
His is a certainty that seems complete,
Seeking nothing he has not already found.

You will see the glow of a holy person
It shines in his flesh.
His body flows in a fluid grace
His rhythm rests in G-d.

So watch him well, sense and know
The peace of one who is sanctified.
Follow closely in his footsteps
They will lead you straight to G-d.

Footprints

In the center of my longings
I find the footprints of Him
   Who walks beside me.
In the midst of my dreams
I see the One who formed
   My sacred visions.

In the dawning of my faith
I will find You,
   My intimate friend.
The life, the source,
The focus of my search
   My Beloved.

Ecstasy

"He who is more than all there is answers with love our trembling awe."

In the Fields

O holy place
Peaceful and serene
Would that I could take with me
The beauty of these mountains,
Painted on the canvas of my heart.

O heat of summer beating down,
Fields fecund and alive.
Singing sun, whispering trees
Moon and stars and desert breath
Faithfully you beckon me:

Be still and know
G-d's presence
In this blessed place.

Erev Shabbat: Snow in Santa Fe

Lord, I am filled with wonder
At the mystery of all things.
The fierce wind blows, the virgin snow swirls
In circles of delight by my window.

Icicles stiff on shuttered doors.
The house resists each growling gust.
What force animates this frozen scene?
What vison forms each graceful part?

The ground is hard, crusty ice holds the logs
Rigid in the woodpile.
Leafless aspens bend and sway,
Surrender to the whistling wind.

Flames sear the beehive hearth,
Flicker on charred walls
Darting, dancing, painting with shadows,
Glowing warmth for body and soul.

Grey smoke escapes its narrow stack
Blends silent with the grey outside.
Night sky glows with unseen sun:
Your promise in nature,
Your echo in the finite world.

Lord, I am struck by Your intricate design,
The mystery of Your creative power.
Cause and effect, force and balance,
All connect on nature's palate;
I glow in awe.

At the River

Dear Lord,

The power of Thy majesty
    blesses this day.
The grandeur of holiness
    fills creation.
The rivers, Lord, the rivers
    lift their voices.

Graceful trees line mossy banks,
    roots reach deep in fertile soil,
The earth, Lord, Thy holy shrine.
    accepts the seed of Thy creation.

They will abound and blossom
    and then grow old, still blooming
As I in life rejoice in prayer
    bursting, echoing Thy praise.
With awe and wonder all my days.

Hasten to Holiness

Soft, warm air surrounds me as I step into
    the breaking dawn.
The sky is cobalt blue.
Stars still dance in the first rays of light
The pungent incense of honeysuckle
    intoxicates.

A single figure etched in the dawn
Stands waiting by the Cardo steps,
Face wreathed in smiles, head wrapped in
    corded scarves.
My friend in faith and faithful friend,
Let's proceed together.

Our steps tap sharply on smooth
    cobbled streets
As we follow a changing path.
Turn here, pass the square,
Down the alleys of Jerusalem stone,
Through the sleeping Jewish quarter.

Hasten to holiness!

Where is that special door?
A glowing smile greets our eager knock.
Come. Come! Enter into your sacred history.
Prepare yourself for the "waters of eden."

Gazing at the gentle waters
Tears of awe catch me unaware.
Cascading down my smiling face,
The millennium of history rolls away.
   "and the spirit of G-d hovered over the
     waters at the beginning of time..."

O the wonder of this moment!

Welcoming arms surround me now, blessing
   my joyous tears.
Warm water closes around my shining body,
Supporting my nakedness of flesh and soul.
To You Hashem, I consecrate my life—
Every breath of my body, every flutter
   of my heart.
                  Kasher!

O the holiness of this moment!

To You Hashem, I dedicate my soul—
Let my heart be pure and my spirit
   watchful.
I am humbled by the sense of
   Your presence.
                  Kasher!

Emerging now, the new day has dawned.
The gentle air of morning echoes the
    rebirth.
A full moon hangs lazily over the Rova roofs,
Gleaming through the deep walled windows.

Birds sing, heralding the moment.
The world glistens, radiant with hope.
What will this new day bring?
How close will I come? How near will You be?

I am here in the service of Your love.

Shining stones, newly washed, ready for
    the tread of day.
Wash away my doubts and fears
Unknowing choices of past years.
Cause the water of Your grace to
    appease my thirst.
I am searching for Your truth
May now be a new beginning.

                              Amen.

Simchat Beit Hasho'evah:
Succot in the Jewish Quarter

Dance in glory, dance in laughter
Hear the happy music of a soulful coronet.
Raise up your children high above
    your shoulders,
Let the generations celebrate with hope.

Dance my children, whirl your praises
Come Jerusalem, put your cares aside.
Dance Jerusalem, now is time for joy.
Celebrate this season, dance your
    night away.

Fire on the Hills

Fire on the hills
Throws its leaping flames
Crimson in the sky.
Blazing tongues, streaking scarlet,
Skip across kissing mountains—
Caress the darkening sky.

Holy fire on the hills,
Now descended once again.
Consuming fire of Your nearness
Inspires my passionate wish
To know You in Your holy mountain.

Fire on the hills,
Sprays its rainbow flames
Orange, vermillion, mandarin, pink
Until the sky is saturated
By Your descent in fire—
The silent herald of Your Being
Constantly beheld.

The Glory of Shabbat Morning

Dazzling light this clear, crisp morning
Showers me with G-d.
The strength of Your love
Pours into my soul
The energy of Your Being
Illuminates my spirit.

Cool breezes splash my face.
The earth breathes strong
Beneath my striding feet.
Safe and sure this day unfolds
Surrounding me as the mountains
       surround Jerusalem.

My skin glistens, my nostrils swell
The scent of sabbath intoxicates.
Every hair, every lash is alive
In this shining moment,
Touched by Your splendor, I am
Robed in the triumph of Your might.

Shabbos Night: Blanket of Stars

Shabbos night, *Shechina's* light
Wrapped tight around the earth,
G-d's blanket of stars
Pulsing,
This shining night in Taos.

The firmament enfolds me,
Holds me, sleeping.
Keeps my dreams warm and bright
This night of stars in Taos.

My dazzled eyes are opened wide
Drinking from Your cup of stars
Glowing with Your holy light.
I am sustained—
This starry night in Taos.

Morning Meditation

The fields form my contemplation
My relation with my soul.
The rain, the sun, the clouds, the clay
They are my daily teachers.
A reminder of Your plan
For man and nature: all is
Order, stillness, surprise.

Hushed voices whisper in the wind
Accompanying the crickets' song,
The scent of stillness hovers,
Perfuming the air and
I am touched, moved by the mystery
Of Your imminence.

The fields are my renewal,
Cleansed by the frost of morning
Gathered into crystal dew.
Your breath, unseen, is everywhere
And You are here in the fields today:
My ecstasy, my inspiration,
My fragrant meditation.

Amen.

Erev Succot

Tomorrow is a golden time
When flames of life flow hot.
When roses grow from stucco walls
And rainbows paint my world.

When birds alight on woven nests
With wiggling worms within their beaks
When sudden showers wash this world
And butterflies fly free.

Tomorrow is a dream inspired
When rivers rise and waters dance,
When I have found Thee all about
And I have felt Thee close.

When prayers consume my questing heart
And gestures of my love abound.
When rhythms of the past release
And life unfolds around my love for Thee.

Filled with G-d

The fire of love
In the souls of men
Loved by G-d
Consumes
Like the fire of G-d's love.
It is the same.

Drawn to one another, we are
Consumed by our hunger
For the supernatural.

Burned by the fire of our
Yearning for G-d
We are carried forward
Into a dialogue of prayer.

Hungry in our pain
The flames of His desire
Fill the emptiness,
And we are swept along
Reaching out
Into the fullness of G-d.

The Power of Prayer

I sense my soul
   carried forward in rapture.
My essential being
   taken up into Yours.
How blessed is the incomprehensible,
    that most intimate
      of human possessions;
Its presence shatters
   my complacency
    filling me with awe.

I honor with silence
   that which transcends reason.
The silken silence
   which envelops the moment
Creating a space for
   the yearning of the heart.
The dreams, the hopes
   the whispers of the soul.
     The possibilities for holiness.

Ignited by G-d

I am a soul ignited by G-d
The corner of a parchment torched by
The flame of His presence.
Curling, changing, moving in response
Touched by just a tiny spark.

An instant of contact is enough
To initiate the sacred process.
The fiery combustion, the fusing
Of wills, one with another
One to touch, one to receive.

Consumed in crackling response
A red hot ember singed by truth,
I am a soul on fire.

Index